PARAPHRASING STRATEGIES

10 Simple Techniques For Effective Paraphrasing In 5 Minutes Or Less

HENRY CHUONG

ISBN: 9781521096178

TABLE OF CONTENT

INTRODUCTION

One of the most common questions my students ask me is *"how can I copy something from a text or paragraph I read that sounds quite good without plagiarism? I'm always tempted to take direct someone else's words from the books I'm reading and put them into my writing, but then I found what I am doing is not allowed; it's called plagiarism. Can you help me solve this problem?"*

Well, one thing that can really help you to copy someone else's ideas or messages without plagiarism is learning how to PARAPHRASING.

As the author of this book, I believe that this book will be an indispensable reference and trusted guide for you who may want to reuse the information of the original text or passage naturally and legally without worrying about plagiarism. Once you read this book, I guarantee you that you will have learned an extraordinarily wide range of useful, and practical paraphrasing techniques that will help you become a successful English writer, particularly in examinations such as Cambridge FCE, CAE, CPE, SAT, TOFEL, and IELTS; as well as you will even become a successful English user in work and in life within a short period of time only.

Thank you for downloading the book *"Paraphrasing Strategies: 10 Simple Techniques For Effective Paraphrasing In 5 Minutes Or Less."*

Let's get started!

What is paraphrasing?

Paraphrasing is simply a restatement of the information of the original text or passage so that it has the same meaning, but in *"your own words"*. The phrase *"in your own words"* indicates that you have to rewrite the original text or passage in your own writing style by using different words. Paraphrasing is an art and a very important skill for writing, speaking, reading and listening. Do it well and nobody will accuse you of plagiarizing. You can represent the same ideas in your own words, but you need to improve the skills to produce good quality rephrasing and rewriting which can effectively help pass the plagiarism checklist.

Here is a quick example of paraphrasing:

The original sentence "Reading is a very important skill for many students."

The paraphrased sentence "For many students, being skillful at reading is extremely important."

Why is it difficult to do paraphrasing?

Sometimes we want to copy something we hear or read that sounds quite good, but we can't do it since it is called copying and it may lead us to plagiarism.

Why Do We Need To Paraphrase? Why Is Paraphrase Important?

Reason 1: Mainly because we want to avoid copying someone else's words; we want to avoid plagiarism.

What is plagiarism?

For example, when I am writing an academic paper in college and I will be reading all kinds of books to get all information I want, then I take direct passages from the books I'm reading and put them into my essay; what I am doing is called plagiarism. It's basically copying someone else's words. It's not allowed; it's illegal.

Reason 2: Another reason why we need to paraphrase is to add a variety of vocabulary and grammatical structures to our writing. Sometimes we may need to repeat some information we put at the beginning of the essay, and we want to use it again to emphasize or whatever reason but we don't want to use the exact same words or the exact same sentence structure as we used before, so we take that information and we write it a different way, but we still keep the same message as the original.

Again, I would like to say that it's really important for you to learn to be able to express something that you've heard or read about in your own words. No worries, I am going to show you some techniques that can help you to paraphrase an original text or passage effectively so as to avoid unintentional plagiarism.

4 Quick and Easy Steps to Effectively Paraphrasing a Text Or Passage.

Step 1: **Read and re-read the original text or passage carefully and make sure you clearly understand what it says.**

This is an important step because you cannot paraphrase what you don't understand. Therefore, you need to read it carefully and you must make sure that you understand it.

If you are not able to fully understand the text or passage since it is too long or boring, then break it up to read it over a few seconds and reread until you understand it completely. Only then you can rephrase the phrases or sentences you want to copy effectively.

Step 2: **Identify the main points and keywords of the text or paragraph.**

Ask yourself the following questions:

  - WHAT is the main idea of the text or paragraph?

  - WHO is the text or paragraph about?

  - WHAT is the text or paragraph about?

  - WHEN does it take place?

  - WHERE does it take place?

  - WHY does it take place?

  - HOW does it take place?

Step 3: **Put away the original text or passage and rewrite it in your own words.**

Make sure to use different vocabulary with the same meaning and change sentence structures/ the order of the words as necessary.

<u>Step 4:</u> Check to see the differences between the original text and what you wrote.

Look at the difference in words and grammar. You can use these tools to help you:

http://handymandanonline.com/Paraphrasing-tool.html

10 Simple Techniques for Effective Paraphrasing

Here are 10 simple techniques you can use when you want to effectively paraphrase something or when you want to express something in your own language.

TECHNIQUE 1: USING SYNONYMS

Synonyms are different words that have the same or similar meanings.

Example 1:

The original sentence "The hardest language to learn is Japanese."

The paraphrased sentence:

- "The most difficult language to learn is Japanese"

- "The most difficult language to be good at is Japanese."

- "The most difficult language to master is Japanese."

Example 2:

The original sentence "Many people in Canada are bilingual",

The paraphrased sentence "Many people in Canada speak two languages".

Example 3:

The original sentence "It can be difficult to choose a suitable website designer from a large number of applicants."

The paraphrased sentence "It is sometimes hard to select an appropriate website designer from many applicants."

Example 4:

The original sentence "Our car needs petrol."

The paraphrased sentence "Our vehicle requires fuel."

Example 5:

The original sentence "Violent crime is on the increase among teenagers."

The paraphrased sentence "Violent offences are increasing among adolescents."

Example 6:

The original sentence "Global warming is mostly caused by emissions from vehicles."

The paraphrased sentence "Climate change is mainly caused by the release of fumes from vehicles."

Example 7:

The original sentence "The school that is across the street is old."

The paraphrased sentence:

- "The school across the street is ancient."

- "The school on the other side of the street is ancient."

Example 8:

The original sentence "There is little chance that my mom will buy me a new PC."

The paraphrased sentence "There is little possibility that my mom will purchase me a new PC."

Example 9:

The original sentence "The Japanese restaurant is located in the city centre of Shanghai."

The paraphrased sentence "The Japanese restaurant is situated in the city centre of Shanghai."

Example 10:

The original sentence "That is a building of 15 floors."

The paraphrased sentence:

- "That is a 15-floor building."

- "That is a building which has 15 floors."

Example 11: LIKE/ LOVE

The original sentence "I enjoy reading comic books."

The paraphrased sentence:

- "I like reading comic books."

- "I love reading comic books."

- "I have a particular liking for reading comic books."

- "I'm fairly/ pretty keen on reading comic books."

- "I'm really into reading comic books."

- "I'm quite a big/ dedicated fan of reading comic books."

- "I'm quite/ pretty fond of reading comic books."

- "I'm totally mad about reading comic books."

- "I'm passionate about reading comic books."

- "I have a strong/clear preference for reading comic books."

- "I'm a great lover of reading comic books."

- "I'm very interested in reading comic books."

Example 12: DISLIKE/ HATE

The original sentence "I don't like living in a big city."

The paraphrased sentence:

- "I don't enjoy living in a big city."

- "I'm not keen on living in a big city."

- "I'm not interested in living in a big city."

- "I hate living in a big city."

- "I can't stand living in a big city."

TECHNIQUE 2: CHANGE THE ORDER OF WORDS

1. If the original sentence has two or more clauses, change the order of the clauses.

Example 1:

The original sentence "If I am late again, my boss will be mad."

The paraphrased sentence "My boss will be mad if I am late again."

Example 2:

The original sentence "If we don't hurry, we will miss the bus."

The paraphrased sentence "We will miss the bus if we don't hurry."

Example 3:

The original sentence "Because Tom slept too late, he missed his first class."

The paraphrased sentence "Tom missed his first class because he slept too late."

Example 4:

The original sentence "In order to pass the final exam, she had to study very hard."

The paraphrased sentence "She had to study very hard in order to pass the final exam."

Example 5:

The original sentence "Tom wanted to buy the car, but he couldn't afford it."

The paraphrased sentence "Tom couldn't afford the car **even though** he wanted it."

<u>Example 6:</u>

The original sentence "Tom had no much money left in the wallet, so he borrowed some."

The paraphrased sentence "Tom borrowed some money **because** he had no much money left in the wallet."

2. If the original sentence has an adjective and noun, change the adjective into a relative clause.

<u>Example 1:</u>

The original sentence "Tom is a very handsome actor."

The paraphrased sentence "Tom is an actor who is very handsome."

<u>Example 2:</u>

The original sentence "Parenting can be a challenging task."

The paraphrased sentence "Parenting can be a task which is challenging."

3. Other cases.

<u>Example 1:</u>

The original sentence "The hardest language to learn is Japanese."

The paraphrased sentence "Japanese **is one of the** most difficult languages to master."

<u>Example 2:</u>

The original sentence "Playing video games too much affects negatively children's poorer health."

The paraphrased sentence:

"Children's poorer health is a negative effect of playing video games."

"Video game players **can** suffer health problems."

"It is believed that playing video games too much has a negative effect on children's health."

"The disadvantage of playing video games is to affect children's health."

"When **children** play video games too much, their health can be negatively affected."

"**Children** play video games too much, **and therefore,** their health may be negatively affected."

Example 3:

The original sentence "Watching films develops people's imagination."

The paraphrased sentence:

"People's imagination development **is a positive effect of** watching films."

"Film watchers **can** develop their imagination."

"It is thought that watching films **is** to develop people's imagination."

"The advantage of watching films **is** to develop people's imagination."

"If people watch films, they can develop their imagination."

"People watch films, **and therefore,** they can develop their imagination."

Example 4:

The original sentence "Peter studied Japanese, **and, as a result,** he translated for our visitors from Japan."

The paraphrased sentence: "Peter could translate for our visitors from Japan, because he had studied Japanese."

TECHNIQUE 3: CHANGE THE FORM OF THE WORD

If the sentence uses a noun, you can rewrite the sentence by using the adverb, adjective or verb form of the word. Change as many words as you can.

Example 1:

The original sentence "In 2012, spending on mobile phones in Australia was around 20 million dollars.

The paraphrased sentence "In 2012, Australian consumers spent around 20 million dollars on mobile phones."

Example 2:

The original sentence "John is an accurate typist."

The paraphrased sentence "John types accurately."

Example 3:

The original sentence "We need to find a solution for this problem."

The paraphrased sentence "We needs to solve this problem."

Example 4:

The original sentence "Diabetes is the cause of kidney disease."

The paraphrased sentence "Diabetes causes kidney disease."

TECHNIQUE 4: USING ANTONYMS, NEGATIVES OR OPPOSITE EXPRESSIONS

Another way to paraphrase is to use antonyms to change a negative expression into a positive expression, or a positive expression into a negative expression.

Example 1:

The original sentence "Tom is short."

The paraphrased sentence "Tom is not tall."

Example 2:

The original sentence "The mall is far away."

The paraphrased sentence "The mall is not near."

Example 3:

The original sentence "Sally was disappointed because the movie was boring."

The paraphrased sentence "Sally wasn't satisfied since the film wasn't very good."

Example 4:

The original sentence "Tom wanted some soup, but there wasn't any in the bowl."

The paraphrased sentence "Tom wanted some soup, but the bowl was empty."

These are examples of using ANTONYMS, NEGATIVES or OPPOSITE EXPRESSIONS to paraphrase phrases or sentences. It is a fairly basic simple technique for us to use once in a while, not all the time, but we can use it successfully.

TECHNIQUE 5: USING A PHRASAL VERB

For example:

Instead of saying "Susan discarded her old watch in the trash bin",

we could say "Susan threw away her old watch in the trash bin".

If we keep using the same words, then it would not be considered "paraphrasing", so what we're looking for is to successfully substitute those words with our own words and also try to resist the temptation of copying or using those words no matter how wonderful they are.

TECHNIQUE 6: CHANGE THE <u>ACTIVE VOICE</u> TO <u>PASSIVE VOICE</u> OR VICE VERSA.

<u>Example 1:</u>

The original sentence "I gave her a watch for her birthday."

The paraphrased sentence "She was given a watch for her birthday."

<u>Example 2:</u>

The original sentence "Someone has cleaned the table."

The paraphrased sentence "The table has been cleaned."

<u>Example 3:</u>

The original sentence "Using mobile phones while driving may cause some serious accidents."

The paraphrased sentence "Some serious accidents may be caused by using cell phones while driving."

TECHNIQUE 7: CHANGE FROM A CLAUSE TO A PHRASE OR VICE VERSA.

Example 1:

The original sentence "After Mary studied, she went to bed."

The paraphrased sentence "After studying, Mary went to bed."

Example 2:

The original sentence "The restaurant across the street is new."

The paraphrased sentence "The restaurant that is across the street is new."

TECHNIQUE 8: CHANGE TRANSITIONS

The original sentence "Although Bob's got a good job, he still complains."

The paraphrased sentence:

"Bob's got a good job, but he still complains."

"Bob's got a good job; however, he still complains."

TECHNIQUE 9: COMBINING OR SEPARATING SENTENCES.

Long sentences can be divided into short sentences, and short sentences can be combined with other short sentences to form long sentences.

Example:

The original sentence "Australia is a wonderful country, which has many beautiful natural landscapes, an interesting history, and friendly people."

The paraphrased sentence:

"Australia is a wonderful country. It has many beautiful natural landscapes, an interesting history, and friendly people."

"Australia, which is a wonderful country, has many beautiful natural landscapes, an interesting history, and friendly people."

TECHNIQUE 10: USING A QUOTATION

Because sometimes we want to copy something we hear or read that sounds quite good, but we can't do it since that is called copying and it may lead us to plagiarism.

Now, what happens if we find a particular phrase or sentence that sounds quite good in our reading passage and we really don't want to paraphrasing or we don't know how to paraphrase it. So what should we do then? Well, in this case, it is possible for us to **use a QUOTATION**. We can use the quotation in a whole sentence and put it in a quotation mark. We could use certain expressions and put them in quotation marks as well.

For example:

"Do the difficult things while they are easy and do the great things while they are small. A journey of a thousand miles must begin with a single step." -- Lao Tzu --

So these are 10 techniques we can use for paraphrasing an original text or passage. This is a really important skill in academic life.

Good luck with your paraphrasing.

VOCABULARY FOR PARAPHRASING WITH EXAMPLES

1. Changes in = trends in
2. Waste output = the amounts of waste

EX: There were considerable changes in/ trends in the amounts of waste produced by all four us companies from 2002 and 2010.

3. The consumption of energy in the United States = the US consumption of energy.

EX: The bar graph compares the consumption of energy in the United States/ the US consumption of energy in 2005.

4. How paper is recycled = the process of paper recycling

EX: The process of paper recycling/ how paper is recycled involves mixing used paper with water and chemicals to break it down.

5. The overall number = the total number

EX: The total number/ the overall number of people participated in this project is 10.

6. Different functions = various features.

EX: There was a significant increase in the number of people using mobile phones for different functions/ various features.

7. The proportion of = the percentage of

EX: The line graph compares the percentage/ proportion of people in five countries who used the Internet from 2000 to 2008.

8. People in the USA = Americans

EX: The proportions of elderly people in the USA/ Americans increased gradually over the period of 20 years.

9. From 2000 to 2008 = between 2000 and 2008 = over a period of 8 years.

EX: The line graph compares the percentage/ proportion of internet users in five countries from 2000 to 2008/ between 2000 and 2008/ over a period of 8 years.

10. How to produce = the process of producing

EX: The diagram illustrates the process of producing/ how to produce electricity in a home using solar panels.

11. In three countries = in the US, Australia and Italy (i.e. Name the countries).

EX: The line graph compares the proportion of people in three countries/ in the US, Australia and Italy who used the Internet between 2000 and 2008.

12. The amount of time spent = the time spent

EX: The bar chart compares the amount of time spent/ the time spent by people in Italy on four different types of phone call between 1999 and 2009.

13. 9 to 14-year-old boys = boys aged between 9 and 14

EX: Boys aged between 9 and 14/ 9 to 14-year-old boys clearly prefer playing on games consoles rather than chatting online.

14. Chatting on the internet = chatting online

EX: The bar chart illustrates the amount of time that 9 to 14-year-old boys spend chatting on the Internet/ chatting online on an average school day in Italy.

15. Playing on games consoles = playing computer games

EX: The bar chart illustrates the amount of time that 9 to 14-year-old boys spend playing on games consoles/ playing computer games on an average school day in Italy.

16. The majority of people = most of the people = most people

EX: Overall, the majority of Canadian people/ most of the Canadian people/ most Canadian people died in a car crash than in a train.

17. Waste paper = paper that has been thrown away.

EX: The diagram illustrates how waste paper/ paper that has been thrown away is recycled.

18. First stage = initial stage
19. Public = individuals
20. Businesses = companies

EX: ...At the first stage/ initial stage of the process, used paper/ waste paper is collected from either public/ individuals or companies/ businesses.....

21. Sort = classify
22. Unsuitable = inappropriate
23. Remove = eliminate = get rid of

EX: ...At the next stage, the paper is classified/ sorted by workers, and inappropriate/ unsuitable paper is eliminated/ removed....

24. Transport = deliver = carry

EX: ... After that, the paper is carried/ transported/ delivered to a paper mill to be ready for the next stages......

25. Criminals = people who commit a crime

EX: People who commit a crime/ criminals should be punished severely.

26. Old people = people who are retired

EX: People who are retired/ old people should be exempt from all taxes.

27. Run their own business = open their own business/ company.

EX: Many young people want to run their own business/ open their own business/ company these days.

28. Start a business = own a business/ company
29. Work for an employer = work for other people

EX: Many young people wants to start a business/ own a business/ company rather than work for an employer/ work for other people.

30. Shopping on the Internet = online shopping = buying/purchasing online

EX: In several countries, online shopping/ shopping on the Internet/ buying/purchasing online is replacing shopping in stores.

31. Sales of fast food = turnover from fast food

EX:

- Sales of fast food/ Turnover from fast food increased from $20 billion in 2002 to over $40 billion in 2012.

- Turnover from fast food increased from $20 billion in 2002 to over $40 billion in 2012.

32. Annual = yearly = per year

EX: The average yearly/ annual spending on medical care per household is approximately $5000.

33. Per person = per capita

EX:

- Consumption of pizza increased to 5 kilograms per person per year.

- The per capita consumption of pizza increased to 5 kilograms per year.

34. Poverty rate = level of poverty = poverty level = the percentage of people who live in poverty.

EX:

- Poverty rate/ level of poverty/ poverty level in India was much higher than that of England.

- The percentage of people who live in poverty in India was much higher than that of England.

35. People who use cars = car users = car commuters = people who commute by car = people who travel by car.

EX:

- The number of car users in 2010 was about 6 million.

- The number of people who use cars in 2010 was about 6 million.

- The number of car commuters in 2010 was about 6 million.

- The number of people who commute by car in 2010 was about 6 million.

- The number of people who travel by car in 2010 was about 6 million.

36. People who cycle to work = cycling commuters

EX:

- Approximately 3 million was the number of people who cycle to work in 2010.

- Around 3 million was the number of cycling commuters in 2010.

37. To rise = to increase = to grow = to go up

EX: Global expenditure on health is predicted to increase/ rise/ grow/ go up to $15.28 trillion worldwide by 2020.

38. A rise = an increase = a growth.

EX: There has been an increase/ a rise/ a growth in the number of people with arthritis and diabetes recently.

39. To decrease = to fall = to drop = to decline = to reduce = to go down

EX: The unemployment tax rate is estimated to decrease/ fall/ drop/ decline/ reduce/ go down by 1% next year.

40. A decrease = a fall = a drop = a decline = a reduction

<u>EX:</u> There has been a decrease/ a fall/ a drop/ a decline/ a reduction in the number of people who are unemployed recently.

PRACTICE

40 ACTIVITIES FOR PARAPHRASING PRACTICE

Paraphrase the following sentences by using your own words:

Activity 1: She is 15 years old.

Activity 2: The percentage of students who used the Internet at the university was about 35%.

Activity 3: The percentage of people who were unemployed in India was around 25% in 2000.

Activity 4: In May, expenditure on mobile phones rose to around $1200.

Activity 5: Approximately 500 people went to his birthday party on Saturday.

About 500 people attended his birthday party on Saturday.

Activity 6: EBay is one of the biggest online shops in the world.

EBay is one of the largest stores on the planet.

Activity 7: The number of seats prepared will be according to the number of guests participating in the event.

Activity 8: Our living room is cleaned by my mom every morning.

Activity 9: Tom will buy a new car tomorrow.

Activity 10: My father's friend loves to make Korean food. He is a professional chef.

Activity 11: Paris has beautiful churches. It's a capital of France.

Activity 12: Sally studied very hard. Her test score was 95%.

Activity 13: You can't play computer games. You have to finish your essay first.

Activity 14: I took pictures of the zebra. The zebra was drinking water from a lake.

Activity 15: Several students are taking pictures of themselves in front of the Harvard University.

Activity 16: Many well-known multinational companies are located in London.

Activity 17: International cooperation is needed to solve the problems resulting from world water scarcity.

Activity 18: Processing mail takes up too much time of many employees.

Activity 19: It is not easy to manage stressful situations.

Activity 20: Information is required to complete a Job Application.

Activity 21: There are many dangers when it comes to teens using drugs.

Activity 22: Being poor often results in a person being broke.

Activity 23: It is illegal to sell heroin in Canada.

Activity 24: Many people do not know the effect of antibiotics.

Activity 25: If he studied hard, he wouldn't fail the exam.

Activity 26: Computers can process information faster and with fewer mistakes than humans.

Activity 27: The process of a large number of people migrating from rural to urban areas in search of work means that the number of hospitals, schools, housing, roading, electricity, and water has to improve.

Activity 28: London is the capital city of England.

Activity 29: A university student usually has a lot of homework to do.

Activity 30: Hidden-video cameras can give people a sense of safety.

Activity 31: The doctors said that he may get cancer if he is not urgently treated.

Activity 32: The police have to put their lives in danger to keep people safe.

Activity 33: The entire city was devastated by the earthquake.

Activity 34: There has been a significant growth in the number of single-person households recently.

Activity 35: The inadequacy of the water supply affects people's health adversely both directly and indirectly.

Activity 36: Only 10% of the college students who have part-time jobs make enough

Activity 37: Rises in the cost of air travel have had a negative effect on tourism.

Activity 38: Pizza is a popular food in America.

Activity 39: She is very talkative.

Activity 40: Tom desires to have a job with high salary.

ANSWERS

Activity 1: She is 15 years old.

The paraphrased sentence:

- She is a 15-year-old.

- She is aged 15.

Activity 2: The percentage of students who used the Internet at the university was about 35%.

The paraphrased sentence:

- The proportion of students using the Internet at the university was about 35%.

- The proportion of students who had access to the Internet at the university was about 35%.

- The proportion of Internet users at the university was about 35%.

Activity 3: The percentage of people who were unemployed in India was around 25% in 2000.

The paraphrased sentence:

- The proportion of people who were jobless in India was around 25% in 2000.

- The unemployment rate in India was around 25% in 2000.

- The proportion of people without job in India was around 25% in 2000.

Activity 4: In May, expenditure on mobile phones rose to around $1200.

The paraphrased sentence: In May, spending on mobile phones increased to around $750.

Activity 5: Approximately 500 people went to his birthday party on Saturday.

The paraphrased sentence: About 500 people attended his birthday party on Saturday.

Activity 6: EBay is one of the biggest online shops in the world.

The paraphrased sentence: EBay is one of the largest online stores on the planet.

Activity 7: The number of seats prepared will be according to the number of guests participating in the event.

The paraphrased sentence: The number of seats prepared will be based on the number of people attending the event.

Activity 8: Our living room is cleaned by my mom every morning.

The paraphrased sentence: My mom cleans our living room every morning.

Activity 9: Tom will buy a new car tomorrow.

The paraphrased sentence: A new car will be bought by Tom tomorrow.

Activity 10: My father's friend loves to make Korean food. He is a professional chef.

The paraphrased sentence: My father's friend, a professional chef, enjoys making Korean food.

Activity 11: Paris has beautiful churches. It's a capital of France.

The paraphrased sentence: Paris, a capital of France, has beautiful churches.

Activity 12: Sally studied very hard. Her test score was 95%.

The paraphrased sentence: Because Sally studied very hard, her test score was 95%.

Activity 13: You can't play computer games. You have to finish your essay first.

The paraphrased sentence: If you don't finish your essay first, you can't play computer games.

Activity 14: I took pictures of the zebra. The zebra was drinking water from a lake.

The paraphrased sentence: While the zebra was drinking water from a lake, I took pictures.

Activity 15: Several students are taking pictures of themselves in front of the Harvard University.

The paraphrased sentence: Quite a few students are taking selfies in front of the Harvard University.

Activity 16: Many well-known multinational companies are located in London.

The paraphrased sentence: Many famous multinational companies are situated in London.

Activity 17: International cooperation is needed to solve the problems resulting from world water scarcity.

The paraphrased sentence: International cooperation is necessary to find solutions for global water scarcity.

Activity 18: Processing mail takes up too much time of many employees.

The paraphrased sentence: Processing mail wastes too much time of many workers.

Activity 19: It is not easy to manage stressful situations.

The paraphrased sentence: The management of stressful situations is difficult.

Activity 20: Information is required to complete a Job Application.

The paraphrased sentence: The completion of information is required on a Job Application.

Activity 21: There are many dangers when it comes to teens using drugs.

The paraphrased sentence: It is dangerous when it comes to adolescents using drugs.

Activity 22: Being poor often results in a person being broke.

The paraphrased sentence: A person who is broke often results from poverty.

Activity 23: It is illegal to sell heroin in Canada.

The paraphrased sentence: Selling heroin in Canada is illegal.

Activity 24: Many people do not know the effects of antibiotics.

The paraphrased sentence: The effects of antibiotics are not known by many people.

Activity 25: If he studied hard, he wouldn't fail the exam.

He wouldn't fail the exam if he studied hard.

Activity 26: Computers can process information faster and with fewer mistakes than humans.

The paraphrased sentence: Computers are more efficient than humans.

Activity 27: The process of a large number of people migrating from rural to urban areas in search of work means that the number of hospitals, schools, housing, roading, electricity, and water has to improve.

The paraphrased sentence: Increased urbanization requires well-developed facilities.

Activity 28: London is the capital city of England.

The paraphrased sentence: The capital city of England is London.

Activity 29: A university student usually has a lot of homework to do.

The paraphrased sentence:

- A person going to university usually has a lot of assignments to do.

- People taking college frequently has a lot of assignments to do.

Activity 30: Hidden-video cameras can give people a sense of safety.

The paraphrased sentence: Hidden-video cameras can make people feel safe.

Activity 31: The doctors said that he may get cancer if he is not urgently treated.

The paraphrased sentence: According to the doctors, he may suffer from cancer if he is not immediately treated.

Activity 32: The police have to put their lives in danger to keep people safe.

The paraphrased sentence: The police have to risk their lives keeping people safe.

Activity 33: The entire city was devastated by the earthquake.

The paraphrased sentence: The earthquake destroyed the whole city.

Activity 34: There has been a significant growth in the number of single-person households recently.

The paraphrased sentence: The number of single-person households has significantly grown these days.

Activity 35: The inadequacy of the water supply affects people's health adversely both directly and indirectly.

The paraphrased sentence: The shortage of the water supply has a negative impact on people's health both directly and indirectly.

Activity 36: Only 10% of the college students who have part-time jobs make enough money to support themselves.

The paraphrased sentence: Of all the students who work part-time, no more than 10% earn sufficient income to make a living.

Activity 37: Rises in the cost of air travel **have** had a negative effect on tourism.

The paraphrased sentence: The tourist industry has been adversely affected by increases in airfare.

Activity 38: Pizza is a popular food **in** America.

The paraphrased sentence: In the United States, many people love to eat pizza.

Activity 39: She is very talkative.

The paraphrased sentence: She is very chatty.

Activity 40: Tom desires to have a job with high salary.

The paraphrased sentence: Tom is such an ambitious person who would like to get a high-paid job.

Conclusion

Thank you again for downloading this book on *"Paraphrasing Strategies: 10 Simple Techniques for Effective Paraphrasing in 5 Minutes or Less."* and reading all the way to the end. I'm extremely grateful.

If you know of anyone else who may benefit from the informative PARAPHRASING tips and techniques presented in this book, please help me inform them of this book. I would greatly appreciate it.

Finally, if you enjoyed this book and feel that it has added value to your work and study in any way, please take a couple of minutes to share your thoughts and post a REVIEW on Amazon. Your feedback will help me to continue to write the kind of Kindle books that helps you get results. Furthermore, if you write a simple REVIEW with positive words for this book on Amazon, you can help hundreds or perhaps thousands of other readers who may want to improve their English writing skills sounding like a native speaker. Like you, they worked hard for every penny they spend on books. With the information and recommendation you provide, they would be more likely to take action right away. We really look forward to reading your review.

Thanks again for your support and good luck!

If you enjoy my book, please write a POSITIVE REVIEW on amazon.

-- Henry Chuong --

Check Out Other Books

Go here to check out other related books that might interest you:

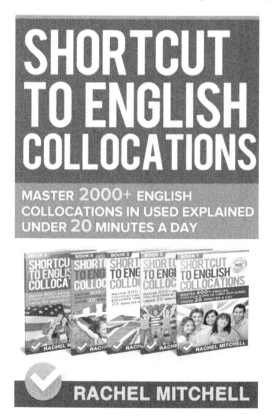

Marriage Heat: 7 Secrets Every Married Couple Should Know On How To Fix Intimacy Problems, Spice Up Marriage & Be Happy Forever

https://www.amazon.com/dp/B01ITSW8YU

Smart Kids Smart Money: The Ultimate Parent's Guide To Teaching
Kids About Earning, Saving, Giving, Spending And Investing Money
Wisely

https://www.amazon.com/dp/B01KEZVFU4

Legal Vocabulary In Use: Master 600+ Essential Legal Terms And
Phrases Explained In 10 Minutes A Day

http://www.amazon.com/dp/B01L0FKXPU

Shortcut To Ielts Writing: The Ultimate Guide To Immediately Increase Your Ielts Writing Scores

http://www.amazon.com/dp/B01JV7EQGG

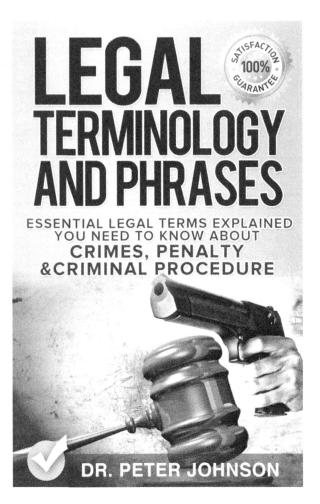

Legal Terminology And Phrases: Essential Legal Terms Explained
You Need To Know About Crimes, Penalty And Criminal Procedure

http://www.amazon.com/dp/B01L5EB54Y

Productivity Secrets For Students: The Ultimate Guide To Improve Your Mental Concentration, Kill Procrastination, Boost Memory And Maximize Productivity In Study

http://www.amazon.com/dp/B01JS52UT6

Daughter of Strife: 7 Techniques On How To Win Back Your Stubborn Teenage Daughter

https://www.amazon.com/dp/B01HS5E3V6

Parenting Teens With Love And Logic: A Survival Guide To Overcoming The Barriers Of Adolescence About Dating, Sex And Substance Abuse

https://www.amazon.com/dp/B01JQUTNPM

Female Organism: The Best Oral Sex Ever To Give Her A Mind-Blowing Pleasure

https://www.amazon.com/dp/B01KIOVC18

GETTING OVER AN AFFAIR

100% SATISFACTION GUARANTEE

5 BIG SECRETS
EXPERTS WANT YOU TO KNOW ON HOW TO
DEAL WITH YOUR PARTNER'S INFIDELITY

JULIE ROSE

http://www.amazon.com/dp/B01J7G5IVS

http://www.amazon.com/dp/B01K0ARNA4

Made in United States
Orlando, FL
02 January 2023